A Forgotte

Mission, Evangelism and the Working Class

Gary Jenkins
Dean of Estates Ministry, Diocese of Southwark

GROVE BOOKS LIMITED
RIDLEY HALL RD CAMBRIDGE CB3 9HU

Contents

Church Mission Society supports the Grove Mission and Evangelism Series
At Church Mission Society, we believe that every Christian is called to join in God's mission, whether that means crossing the street or crossing continents, and we want to set people free to put that call into action.

Dedication
To the people of St James and St Anne's, Bermondsey

First Impression November 2024
ISSN 2399-6536
ISBN 978 1 78827 431 9

1

A Forgotten People

2025 marks the fortieth anniversary of the publication of the seminal report *Faith in the City: A Call for Action by Church and Nation* from the Archbishop of Canterbury's Commission on Urban Priority Areas.[1] It noted then:

> The Church of England's most enduring 'problem of the city' has been its relationship with the urban working class.[2]

Forty years on the challenge remains, although in the last decade there have been growing signs of a renewed interest in urban mission, in work on social housing estates and low-income communities and in the issue of class.[3]

The mission challenge is huge. Working-class people (however defined) make up a large, neglected and often forgotten group in the population. Working-class culture is frequently viewed in negative terms, with a focus on its problems and weaknesses, especially in the most socially deprived communities.

But what are the positives of working-class culture, and what are the biblical resonances with it? What methods, strategies and presentations of the gospel can enable a mainly middle-class church to engage in cross-cultural mission to and with working-class people? How can working-class people be equipped for leadership and mission in the church? How can the church receive their gifts? The book will aim to address these issues.

There is the danger of stereotyping. What may be said of a group generally may not apply to all. Nonetheless there are recognizable patterns that can be discerned in communities and cultures and it is helpful to consider these in order to enable mutual understanding and to engage profitably in mission. In that spirit, I offer these thoughts as a personal view from my own experience of growing up in a working-class family, from ministry in four south London parishes, and from my present role as Dean of Estates Ministry in the Diocese of Southwark.[4] I aim to offer an affectionate but not uncritical view of the people from whom I come.

Who are Working-class People?

Some people think they no longer exist.

It is suggested today that either *no one* is working class and, therefore, the term is an anachronism, or *everyone* is working class and therefore the term is meaningless. Although precise definitions are difficult, most working-class people react positively to the term and even embrace it with pride (a favourite working-class term—see below).

Some use the term too narrowly to refer only to the very poorest and most vulnerable in society, the people who, in one social classification, are referred to as 'the precariat' ('the most deprived class of all with low levels of economic, cultural and social capital').[5] The most enduring classification of social class employed in the UK, however, is that produced by the National Reader Survey which divides the population into the following six social grades:[6]

Class	Occupations	% of UK population in 2016
A	Higher managerial, administrative and professional	4
B	Intermediate managerial, administrative and professional	23
C1	Supervisory, clerical and junior managerial, administrative and professional	28
C2	Skilled manual workers	20
D	Semi-skilled and unskilled manual workers	15
E	State pensioners, casual and low-grade workers, unemployed with state benefits only	10

Grades C2, D and E, which make up 45% of the population, comprise the working class. It is this group that is the concern of this booklet. This is a large group in society. It includes the poor, but not just the poor. It includes those with few or no academic qualifications, although many working-class people are highly trained and highly skilled. It includes families that are broken and in disarray, although many working-class families are together and function well.

Class is an important issue for the church to think about in terms of its mission 'to all people everywhere' (Matt 28.19 (GNB)). The working class are a missiologically discrete but diverse group, with particular values and outlooks on life. In any work of mission, it is important to take seriously matters of culture, but especially so in the case of working-class people because the church so often is a predominantly middle-class institution. Working-class people can be overlooked or problematized or the victim of stigma and prejudice.

Dagenham-born trade unionist Paul Embery has written about 'why the modern left loathes the working class.' He argues that the Labour Party has lost touch and sympathy with working-class people. He maintains that, though it is a diverse group, 'There is a common thread running through most of the working class—one that is patriotic, often socially conservative, communitarian, rooted, and which places a high value on family, place, social solidarity and cultural stability.'[7]

Embery is a member of the Blue Labour movement whose leader, Maurice Glasman, believes that Labour has largely rejected the leadership of working-class people.[8] For the church, another institution with a weak connection with the working class, some of the analysis coming from Blue Labour writers is very pertinent to our own situation.

The church is run by middle-class people for middle-class people and it thinks, operates and communicates in middle-class ways, almost without realizing it. The gospel is viewed from a middle-class perspective and is framed in ways that appeal to middle-class people and answer the questions they have. Paul Brown describes his early experience as a Christian as encountering an alien culture:

> When I...first walked into a church meeting it was difficult to find people like me. People with similar values and interests, a similar accent and job. I quickly realized that this church was very middle class: middle-class attitudes, middle-class values and middle-class social circles all dominated. I have learnt over the years that my initial experience of church is far from unique. In fact, the dominant culture of the church in the UK typically reflects a middle-class life.[9]

Similarly, a recent study found Church of England clergy from a working-class background experienced 'discomfort and feelings of alienation manifest in different ways but often described as a vague sense of being out of place.'[10]

Working-class people are overlooked because they are a very small group *within most congregations* and unrepresented in most church structures. They are overlooked because many live on estates which are geographically distinct and separate from the surrounding community. They are overlooked because they have proved difficult to reach and incorporate into the life of a largely middle-class church. They are overlooked when a church focusing too much on results goes for the easier to reach groups: students (in particular), some minority groups, and middle-class families.

They are overlooked because of (largely unspoken) prejudice towards working-class people. They are overlooked because they are seen as racists or the holders of unpopular opinions, for example, voting for Brexit, or believing that council houses *should* be sold to their occupants.[11] They are the white van men. They are the people who display England flags on their houses or cars. They are proud of their country. They feel strangely victimized and they cannot work out why.

Very often the working class are simply absent from the church and its councils. They are not there to plead their cause, and few others are prepared to speak on their behalf and perhaps even fewer are prepared to listen. It is strange that so little recognition is given of that fact that the working class of England is so sparsely represented not just in the national church's leadership, but in its congregations, too.[12]

In my last parish the local football team, Millwall, famously has the slogan 'Nobody likes us and we don't care.' This may say something about the (somewhat undeserved) reputation of Millwall fans but to turn the disdain of your detractors on its head by chanting 'Nobody likes us' with a kind of pride is a wonderful piece of working-class defiance and humour.

Of course, really, they *do* care and they are furious about it.

2

Fun, Family and Solidarity

We now turn to consider some of the key attributes of working-class culture, both its strengths and its shadow side. Of course, there is the danger of stereotyping. Inevitably I am painting with broad brushstrokes, making generalizations about a large and diverse group in our society, but I aim to give something of the *flavour* of working-class culture seen from the perspective of my own experience of growing up in a working-class family.

Family

People generally love their families but the family has a special place in working-class culture because it is the heart of the understanding of the *meaning* of what life is all about. If the average working-class person is asked to speak about what matters to them most and, crucially, what gives their life meaning, they are most likely to speak about their family. Middle-class people are most likely to speak of their occupation, their education or their hobbies, their interests or their achievements,

This comes out powerfully in working-class funeral eulogies which are full of stories about the character and the foibles of the deceased, not so much their achievements, but the kind of person they were and, especially, what they meant to their loved ones. One of the most noticeable features of the many large and elaborate funerals in my south London working-class parish was the men *crying*. All this speaks of the value of family and of a culture that, at its best, is warmly expressive and affectionate.

Working-class culture is a people-centred culture and so are the newspapers and TV programmes that working-class people typically connect with. The tabloid press is full of human-interest stories as are some of the most popular TV programmes in working-class areas such as the soaps with their stories of everyday lives in communities and families, and many reality TV programmes.

Collectivism

In the face of Western culture that is deeply individualist, working-class culture values the group over the individual. The quintessential working-class institution is the trade union whose *raison d'etre* is to foster collective action on behalf of the group. A noticeable feature of testimonies given by working-class people is the inclusion of the church as part of the blessings of the gospel. They value the personal sense of salvation and commitment to Jesus Christ as Lord and Saviour as much as all Christians but it is characteristic of working-class testimonies to say something along the lines of 'I have a wonderful saviour in Jesus and I have a new wonderful family in the church.' By contrast church membership is rarely included in middle-class testimonies. It is not denied but it is not thought of being included in a testimony because the person is understood to be speaking about their *individual* experience and *individual* connection with God and so the church drops out of view.

Connected to the importance of the group is the idea of working-class solidarity, of standing with someone, of being on their side and by their side. It is about sticking together through thick and thin. Loyalty to the group and especially the family is very important. The home I grew up in was a very loving and secure home. There was one rule that my parents emphasized we must always follow: 'You must always be loyal to your family.' This, to me, is the very essence of working-class culture.

All of this finds ready echoes in Blue Labour thinkers such as Paul Embery who (as we have already seen) suggests that working-class communities are 'patriotic, often socially conservative, communitarian, rooted,' placing a high value on 'family, place, social solidarity and cultural stability.'[13]

Acceptance

Arising out of the value given to the group and family, the people-centered nature of working-class culture can be very warm and accepting. 'Make yourself at home' is a great working-class phrase that speaks strongly of love and acceptance. Clergy visiting working-class homes to arrange a funeral have often remarked that by the end of the visit that they feel as if they are part of the family. One of the first black women to enter a working-class church in south London in the 1960s was greeted by a white woman who said, 'You come and sit with me, love.'[14] Forty years later she is still a member of that church. One of the features of working-class speech is that they use your name a lot when they speak to you. I particularly notice this on funeral visits. Also, terms of affection are promiscuously deployed even to complete strangers: 'love,' 'darling,' 'sweetheart,' 'babe' and, of course, 'mate.'[15]

Pride

In working-class culture pride is a key word and a key concept.

Pride gets a bad press in the Bible. In Christian theology it is one of the seven deadly sins.

In working-class culture, the word is used more positively. First, it is about expressing approval and appreciation in someone or something. When a vicar was having a hard time in the parish his working-class churchwarden, as well as sending him a bottle of wine, sent a text message saying, 'We're proud of you.'

It is about being proud of the job you do, the place where you live, your family, your country and its history. A General Synod debate that sought to address the plight of refugee professionals bemoaned the fact some of these individuals had to be taxi drivers or cleaners—as if these were dishonourable occupations. The Church of England's very middle-class assembly seemed innocent of the fact that some people are *proud* to be taxi drivers. The cause of the refugees could have been advanced without talking down the jobs of working-class people.[16]

Secondly, it is deeply rooted in the sense of self-worth.

'I've got my pride,' someone says. It is pride that has been dented by many well-intentioned middle-class efforts to 'help the poor.' Middle-class Christians on the whole enjoy helping the poor more than the poor enjoy being helped. Although 'the poor' may be grateful for the help given, they hate being in the situation where they need that help. The findings of focus groups looking at poverty found radically different understandings of poverty. The middle-class groups saw poverty in material terms, the absence or lack of money or decent housing, financial security. The working class spoke of what it *felt* like to be poor. Repeatedly they spoke of 'shame, inferiority, powerlessness, humiliation, fear, hopelessness, depression, social isolation and voicelessness.'[17]

Being poor made them feel bad about themselves, because they were unable to provide for themselves and, especially, for their family. Any effort to help the poor needs to take into account this factor, not add to the shame, not inadvertently deepen the gulf between the working-class person and the church. For example, Lupton suggests a series of 'Oaths for Compassionate Service' which include:

- Never do for the poor what they have (or could have) the capacity to do for themselves
- Limit one-way giving to emergency situations
- Strive to empower the poor through employment, lending and investing
- Subordinate self-interests to the needs of those being served
- Listen closely to those you seek to help, especially to what is not being said[18]

Fun

Life is to be enjoyed: away with deferred gratification, let's enjoy life now! 'You only live once' is another great working-class saying. If you have got money, spend it. And enjoy it. Of course, working class people have their full share of the sorrows of life but they enjoy life and they like fun. They particularly enjoy having a laugh. Humour is a key ingredient of all working-class events, even including funerals (perhaps, especially funerals). What people most enjoy is funny stories about people they know—because people are endlessly fascinating (and comical). Whatever you may think of his politics (or his character) what endeared Boris Johnson to some working-class people is that he did not appear to take himself too seriously. He seemed to be a laugh.

The Shadow Side

Every culture has its shadow side and that is true of working-class culture as much as any other. Here are a few:

- *Feuds*: It is one of the paradoxes that a culture that is very strong on love and acceptance can also be peculiarly unforgiving. It can be very difficult for people to back down, admit they are wrong or to offer an olive branch of forgiveness. This is one of the causes of the long-standing feuds that are feature of many working-class communities and families. 'I'll never speak to him again' is a phrase that is often heard. People prefer to walk away rather than work for compromise or reconciliation.
- *A fragile sense of self-worth* can be one of the features of working-class culture that holds people back in all kinds of ways. 'I wouldn't be able to do this' can be the default response to a new challenge and the repeated thought nags inside: 'I'm not good enough.' They often lack confidence and tend to underestimate themselves. The fragile sense of self-worth may also be at the heart of the anger, the bitterness, the tantrums and the walkings away that occur in working-class communities. What appears to be a disproportionate response to a perceived slight comes from a deep hurt and a sense of self-worth, already fragile, that has been seriously injured.
- *The relationship to the church and matters of faith*. Generally speaking, working-class people believe in God and the afterlife. Atheism and agnosticism seem to be a more middle-class preoccupation. The God that many working-class people believe in is a distant but tolerant deity ('him upstairs') who you can turn to in a moment of crisis but who will not unduly trouble you on a day to day basis.

The afterlife is 'the big pub in the sky,' that is, just like this life but better. Heaven, if it is anything, is a family reunion. Increasingly, as newspaper obituaries and eulogies show, many people believe that the departed become stars or angels after death. 'Nanny has gained her wings' is the latest euphemism for death. Children will be taken out to view the night sky and to see Granny's star shining in the night sky. Tim Rice may have set this ball rolling with the line: 'There's one more angel in heaven, there's one more star in the sky.'[19] This is a long way from a Christian understanding of the life of the world to come.

Working-class people like the church but do not see themselves as part of it, so far as church attendance goes. Winston Churchill once said, 'I am not a pillar of the church. I am more of a flying buttress: I support it from the outside.' This is pretty much the approach of many working-class people—supportive—from the outside. Hayley Humphries in her (unpublished) dissertation, *'What are the perceptions of God and the church on an urban outer estate, and what are the implications for mission?'* found on the estate where she serves there was an openness towards God and 'a fondness and appreciation towards the church' among non-churchgoers.

There are a number of things about the church that makes working-class people feel either they would not be welcome or they would not enjoy church: (1) they are not good enough; (2) people like them do not go there; (3) church is too cold. The last point is the most important.

It is not the physical temperature that puts people off (though that does not help) but the emotional temperature. Church feels formal and distant, a far cry from the warmth, humanity and intimacy of a working-class family. Church lacks emotional warmth, as working-class people see it. This perception is not helped by the fact that the church services that they go to most often, such as weddings, baptisms and funerals, are the more formal occasions. However welcoming the church may be on these occasions, working-class visitors know this is not a group that they really belong to. Evidence of this is that for all these occasional offices, people will wait outside the building (even in freezing cold weather or driving rain) for a chat and a laugh and will only go inside at the very last minute. They will also be the first to leave. At the end it will not just be the smokers who will be breathing a sigh of relief that it is over and they can go outside. The reality of the local church, Sunday by Sunday for an actual member of a congregation may be rather different, but what people *think* it will be like may be enough to stop them coming.

If these are some of the strengths and weaknesses of working-class culture, what are some of the Christian resonances with it? It is to that we now turn.

3 Christian Resonances

The gospel stands in judgment on all cultures including working-class culture. Aspects of that culture, as much as any other culture, need to be challenged and changed by the transforming power of the gospel (although there has been a tendency for the church to be harder on working-class sins than middle-class ones).

What are the Christian concepts, values, practices and presentations of the gospel that resonate with working-class culture? What challenges are offered to working-class culture by the gospel and what is the good news for it? It is to these questions that we now turn.

The connections with working-class culture: as we have seen, there is a tendency to speak of working-class culture in terms of its problems and deficiencies, partly because of the focus on social deprivation and the lives of the most troubled and needy families. These challenges must not be overlooked but it is worth considering what is good about working-class culture, what aspects of it are in harmony with biblical teaching, and what aspects of it may be closer to the Bible's understanding of the good life and the good community than that held by the middle-class culture that predominates in most churches.

A number of biblical themes find a ready echo in working-class culture

A number of biblical themes find a ready echo in working-class culture: the focus on the collective rather than the individual, on acceptance, on joy, on solidarity and loyalty. The Bible takes the individual seriously but most of Scripture is the story of a people. The epistles are mainly addressed to a group. In English versions of the Bible the word 'you' often translates the second-person plural and not the second-person singular (as Western Christians instinctively read it). A Liverpudlian preacher once pointed out that he had an advantage, that he had a word for the second-person plural that distinguished it from the singular: *yous*. How different our reading of Scripture would be if we could say 'yous' or at least remind ourselves that the group rather the individual is being addressed in the first instance in many cases, especially in most of the epistles.

Solidarity and loyalty matter to working-class people and these themes are echoed throughout Scripture. It is the 'steadfast love' of the Lord that never ceases (Lam 3.22–23). It is the covenant loyalty of Ruth that leads her to assure her bereaved mother-in-law, 'Where you go I will go, and where you stay I will stay' (Ruth 1.16) and it is the utterly reliable, faithful, and steadfast God who says, 'I will be their God, and they shall be my people' (Heb 8.10).

Working-class people value fun, enjoyment, celebration and laughter. The essential Christian message is one of 'good news of great joy' (Luke 2.10). God's salvation brings joy and laughter (Ps 126.2). A church that can express that joy, that knows how to celebrate, that is full of laughter will find a ready connection with working-class people.

The focus on acceptance in working-class culture finds a ready echo in the biblical themes of forgiveness, justification, adoption and the universal offer of the gospel. Chris Arnade in his book, *Dignity: Seeking Respect in Backrow America,* perfectly captures this as he describes the accepting welcome of an American working-class church that contrasts with the experience that 'backrow Americans' have of the various civil and social institutions they also encounter in the rest of their lives:

> There are rules to follow if you join, but they don't require having your paperwork in order, having proper ID. They don't require getting grilled about this and that. They say 'Enter as you are,' letting forgiveness wash away a past that many want gone. You are welcome as long as you try. The churches understand the streets, understand that everyone is a sinner, and everyone fails. In their minds, the rest of the world—the courts, the hospitals, the rehab clinics, the welfare office, police stations and even some of the nonprofits and schools...doesn't understand them. The cold, secular world of the well-intentioned is a distant and judgmental thing. The world has given them seemingly nothing but pain[20]

The challenges to working-class culture: the sense of the group solidarity *and* the high focus on loyalty to the group is both a strength and a weakness of the culture. It makes it difficult to be different or to stand out from the crowd or to be disloyal to the values of the group. In some cases, this makes it hard for working-class people to fully commit themselves to the faith of Christ and to active membership of the church. The kingdom calls people to leave aspects of our old life behind, to follow Christ, to make new allegiances and to live a different life (Eph 4.17). Christ calls his people to be in the world but not of it (John 17.14–16). It is particularly difficult to stand out from the crowd if you are the only Christian in your family and the sense of loyalty and commitment to the family is very strong. That is an experience far more common for working-class Christians than middle-class ones, because of the paucity of working-class Christians in most places.

A further challenge to working-class culture comes in the area of unforgiveness, of the long-term feud, of the reluctance to back down or to seek reconciliation. By contrast Christians are called to repent of their own sins (1 John 1.8–10), to forgive those who persecute or harm them (Eph 4.31–32) and to work for reconciliation (Matt 5.9). At this point the gospel offers a radical challenge to working-class culture.

The good news for working-class culture: paradoxically what is the biggest stumbling block for working-class people in encountering the Christian faith is, or at least can be, part of the good news for them. For all its failings, the church is God's family. It is God's dearly loved people and working-class converts, as we have already seen, often have such an appreciation of the joy of joining that family that they often include it in their story of faith.

An apologetic for the church can be a crucial part of reaching working-class people

Working-class people who do join the church often find it is a better experience than they feared it would be. For this reason, an apologetic for the church can be a crucial part of reaching working-class people for the gospel. We do not need to feel ashamed of the church or apologize for it, but we do need to offer an apologetic for it, in the sense of offering a defence and explanation that will make sense to working-class people and help them to overcome one of the chief obstacles to their wholehearted participation in the life of God's kingdom. Newbigin is right: 'The only hermeneutic of the gospel, is a congregation of men and women who believe it and live by it'.[21]

Anything that can dispel the rather dour and forbidding image that people have of the church, anything the church can do to express the joy, celebration and warmth of the gospel, and any stepping stones that the church can create, small steps into faith and into membership of the church, will be an important part of the process of commending the faith to working-class people. The psalmist says 'Taste and see that the Lord' is good (Ps 34.8). We need the boldness to say the same about the church.

For a culture that has a problem with unforgiveness, long-running feuds and backing down, the gospel offers a new and better way forward: God's way, of forgiveness, of relationships restored, of reconciliation. Broken things can be made new, including relationships. The cycle of unforgiveness and bitterness can be broken by the power of God's love. You do not have to walk away or walk out. You can come back. You do not have to 'never speak again.' Instead, words of peace can be spoken and cherished and damaged relationships can be renewed. This is part of the good news to and for working-class culture.

The worth and value of the individual in creation and redemption is an important point for any person to grasp, but particularly one prone to a low sense of self-worth who has been put down, under-appreciated, or made the victim of prejudice. The supreme value and dignity of every human being is rooted in our creation in the 'image and likeness of God.' The church of God, meaning the people of God, is precious in his eyes because it was 'bought with his own blood' (Acts 20.28). As I have argued elsewhere, a substitutionary understanding of the atonement has a particular resonance for working-class people, because it speaks of the price that was paid by the saviour, of the value of a life for which the Son of God gave his life.[22] This is what a man from a south London council estate understands about this:

> It's knowing your sins are paid for, having assurance. It's freedom—from the guilt. The guilt used to play over in my head but now I can come to the cross and confess it and Jesus will take it on himself. When I think of the cross, I think of the pain he was prepared to endure for me. He did it 2000 years ago but he has done it for us now[23]

4 Connecting with Working-class Culture

We turn now to consider specific ways of connecting with working-class culture and people. What are the effective points of contact? What strategies actually work? What evangelistic messages and what types of church and church activity connect best? How can the church work with and alongside working-class people in the work of mission?

One of the most effective ways of seeking to reach working-class people for the gospel is intentionally to create an indigenous working-class church, rooted in the culture, which resonates with that culture. The Church of England's estates evangelism strategy has the aim of creating 'loving, worshipping, serving communities on every significant estate in the nation.'[24] It is a classic 'go to' rather than 'come to us' strategy.

To the objection that an intercultural church is a better reflection of the biblical ideal, exemplified by the eschatological gathering of people from every 'nation, tribe, people and language' (Rev 7.9), the point needs to be made that it is not always possible when the actual area that the church serves is mainly or exclusively working class (as is frequently the case with churches serving large local authority estates). It is not always possible when the middle-class nature of the church is so entrenched and pervasive that the only realistic way of incorporating working-class people into the life of the church is by an entirely fresh expression of church. It is not enough simply to state, 'Everyone is welcome here' if a particular section of the community is significantly underrepresented or not represented at all.

On his visits to learn from the citizens of 'backrow America,' Wall Street banker Chris Arnade often found himself in churches which (alongside branches of McDonalds) were the places where 'backrow people' were most likely to gather. Arnade is an atheist but he listens sympathetically. He begins to understand why the churches he visits connect with backrow America:

> They walk inside the church and immediately they meet people who get them. The preachers and congregants inside may preach to them and even judge their past decisions, but they don't look down on them. They have walked the walk and know the shit they are going through… from their own lives or the lives of their friends. They look like them and they get them.[25]

He vividly describes one service in a small storefront church: 'Everyone in attendance takes a turn at the front either singing, reading, preaching or chanting.' A man walks round 'calling out Scriptures like an auctioneer,' children read out little 'speeches handwritten on lined paper,' a man says 'I used to drink all the time until I discovered the Lord…I've been free from booze for fourteen years' and a woman tells the congregation 'I have had it rough, but with you and the Lord, I will keep my head up high' and then three women sing:

> Get up, get up, get up in Jesus' name!
> The Lord is calling daily to those who would be saved
> Don't go down defeated while victory's here to claim
> Get up, get up, get up in Jesus' name.[26]

This is a church full of hope. It also suggests an indigenous church, a church of the people, for the people.

Far too often, however, working-class converts have been expected to integrate with middle-class culture. Paul Brown describes his first experience of church on coming to faith:

> …church was achingly middle class. The people didn't dress like me, they didn't talk like me, they didn't socialize like me. The jobs they did and how they spent their money was so different from me. Even the humour they used was different; nothing was the same.[27]

What might a more authentically working-class church look like?

Wednesday Night Church in the parish of St James, Bermondsey is one possible response to this challenge. It takes place every Wednesday night with three basic ingredients: some food, some Bible and worship. The first hour is eating and chatting. Then there is Bible input. A variety of options have been used; perhaps the best is for the Sunday preacher to give a shortish précis of Sunday's sermon followed by discussion around the tables. This leads on to some concluding songs. The advantages are that people get to know one another well. It is relaxed and informal. There is definite Bible input focused at a level and in a style that will connect with those there. One of the striking aspects is the number of non-Sunday churchgoers, especially men, who have found a home here. The gathering is probably 50/50 of Sunday church members and non-Sunday church members. Many are working-class people from the surrounding estates. It works for them. It resonates with their culture. It is relational. It is strong on acceptance. It has a family feel. It is warm and it is fun.

There is no one style of worship or preaching that will unfailingly connect with working-class people. Worship and preaching that is clear, direct, collective, with emotional impact, that relates to human life will be important. Not abstract or academic. Or boring.

Resources for Mission

Most courses and programmes designed to communicate the gospel to outsiders are designed with middle-class people in mind. Those ministering in working-class areas have the choice of either adapting the material or using material as it stands which does not quite fit or connect. It is one of the many ways those ministering to working-class people are placed at a disadvantage even before they start. However, a small number of courses and programmes have been specifically designed with 'ordinary people' in mind and have a proven track record in working-class churches and amongst working-class people. Here are four of them:

- *Jesus Shaped People:* According to the programme's website: 'Jesus Shaped People has not come from a classroom or a college, but a parish church on one of the toughest and most disadvantaged estates in the North of England.'[28] It is more than just a course, more a whole church programme designed to revitalize the church's life.
- *The Start Course* hails from the north of England, is filmed on location there and is deliberately designed to connect with working-class people with vox pop interviews and settings including Blackpool beach, a fun fair, a shopping centre and a junk yard.[29]
- *Simply Christianity* has been used successfully in urban and estate settings. It has the advantage of being not too long, and of simplicity of presentation with minimal addition resources required.[30]
- *The Urban Catechism* is written by Duncan Forbes for use on the Alton Estate in south London and is described as 'a discipleship tool...specifically written with council estates and deprived areas in mind.'[31] The catechism follows Forbes' own Reformed evangelical theological commitments, but the use of the idea of a catechism as a teaching tool for ministry to urban people is an interesting one and could be adapted to other theologies.

A further resource is provided by the *Proximity online hub* which seeks to (1) raise 'awareness of the disconnect between the church and those living in low-income communities; (2) 'resource and support Christians living and ministering in urban contexts' and (3) 'by sharing the stories of those involved in urban ministry…highlight best practice and share key learning.'[32] As well as offering a wealth of free resources, Proximity aims to create an online and in-person community for encouraging and equipping those engaged in urban mission.

The most important resource for mission to working-class communities is working-class Christians themselves—people who know the area they live in and the culture from which they come, people who have a certain credibility in their community and speak the language of those to whom they minister.

Connecting Through Digital Outreach

During lockdown in my south London parish of St James and St Anne Bermondsey, in addition to normal online Sunday services we experimented with a series of specials that were specifically designed to communicate with those outside the church. They were shared on social media. We were aiming for a magazine format a bit like the BBC *One Show*. Thirty to thirty-five minutes was the maximum length. There were hymns and songs, Bible readings read by members of the congregation on location around the community, a short talk, testimonies and interviews. Christmas, Harvest, Easter and Mothering Sunday were obvious choices, but the runaway success was the Valentine's community video. For Valentine's Day we asked people via Facebook who had been married at St James or St Anne to send in their wedding photos. Many people did, allowing the video to conclude with a photo montage of Bermondsey weddings through the ages as the Wedding March played in the background.

The location was crucial. Working-class culture has a strong sense of the local and of place. People like seeing the places they knew (the school, the marketplace, the doctor's surgery, the allotments, the local Co-op) and the people they knew. For the Christmas carol service, we had the lessons read by people at their place of work: the MP in his office, the funeral directors at the funeral parlour, the fishmonger at the fish stall, and the head teacher in the school playground.

The series concluded with a special video, *Bermondsey Proud and Thankful*, celebrating the local community, introduced by the curate from the top of the church tower surveying the community below. This included a trip down the river in a Port of London Authority vessel with the deputy harbourmaster (a member of the congregation), a visit to Millwall Football Club to hear about their work in the community, a visit to a food bank run by a black majority church, and an interview with a stall holder at the local market, concluding with a photo montage of local community celebrations as the words of the blessing were sung, 'The Lord bless you and keep you.'

In short, the videos were designed to be celebratory, fun, connected with the locality and with a clear but simple Christian message in each case. Although these were low-budget productions with fairly minimal advertising, the number of people who watched them was way beyond the numbers who ever attended our services.[33] There could be scope for a national project aimed to connect with working class people via video.

Indigenous Leadership

One of the challenges of a creating a church that intentionally includes working-class people concerns the selection and training of people for leadership, both ordained and lay.

For the mission of the church one of the best ways of communicating to people of a particular culture is to have someone from that culture who knows it from the inside and speaks the right cultural language. This is an important for working-class culture as for any other culture. Paul Brown comments:

> If we truly want to change church culture and reach the neglected communities in the UK, one of the things we urgently need to change is how we define what makes a good leader…There seems to be a lack of leaders who are willing and able to reach out into working-class communities. And there is undoubtedly a lack of leaders who identify as working class.[34]

Clearly cross-cultural mission is always possible. Indeed, many middle-class leaders have been outstandingly effective in working-class contexts. Nonetheless, the challenge of an indigenous leadership remains. It is important for working-class people to see people like themselves in leadership, and for their gifts and abilities to be employed in the life of the church and not to be overlooked.

Michael Leyden has observed:

> For those of us who come from urban estates, the process towards recognized public ministry can feel very alien; it has often required leaving some key identity markers behind…to take up cultural habits and behaviours that are more typically (middle class) 'church leader shaped'.[35]

In the light of this a welcome recent development in a number of Church of England dioceses has been the creation of training pathways for people from low-income communities and estates communities. The aim is to equip and train people to minister to people like themselves in their home community using an experience-based participatory style of learning, in order to draw upon the gifts and skills of those who have few if any academic qualifications, but wide experience of life. They form the rare instance of materials and courses being produced with the non-tertiary educated half of the population in mind.

Church Army's research unit has researched and evaluated a number of courses that have been specifically designed to address the question: 'How can the Church of England identify, resource, and enable people who live on urban estates to be relationally effective in leadership, mission, and evangelism?'[36] Not all working-class people live on estates but most people who live in socially-rented accommodation on estates are working class.

Five courses have been studied and evaluated: *MPower* (Blackburn); *Stepping Up* (York); *Become* (London); *Local Ministry Pathway* (Birmingham); *Church Army Initial Training*.

They have a number of points in common: *adaptation* (the flexibility and adaptability necessary to the unpredictable and messy nature of life on many urban estates); *authenticity* (led by people with significance experience of urban ministry, seeking to create a culture where people can be honest and real with each other); *building confidence*, which seems to be the most crucial ingredient of all because people arrive on the course typically hugely lacking in confidence in themselves and unconvinced about their participation; *a flexible approach to assessment and learning activities* (through the use of journaling, take-home activities, in-session reflective exercises and the option of recorded conversations instead of written work) and *the involvement of the local church* in selection, support and deployment.

Rejecting the charge that such courses might represent a dumbing down or a lowering of standards, Canon Andy Delmege from the Birmingham course states:

> This is not a second-best way of training; rather it is one that forms the people that God is calling from these contexts to minister effectively and missionally within them[37]

Each course is customized to local needs. There is no one-size-fits-all model. Each course sets out to create a learning community and places an emphasis on building close and trusting relationships. Each course involves a significant investment of time and energy both by the sponsoring bodies and the participants, though the feedback is overwhelmingly that this investment is worth it.[38].

Some of the responses of group members are telling:[39]

- It gave me the chance to meet people like me, not middle class, but in similar situations
- I grew in confidence to be a leader—to talk to people, to pray with people
- Confronting any fears, *eg* 'Am I good enough?'
- Gain more confidence speaking in front of others. To apply for a care worker job. To listen to people better. To understand the needs of others better
- Doing the course gave me confidence I never had before and I liked being able to put what I learned into practice
- We learned how anyone can be a leader—there are so many different types—I could begin to see myself as a leader
- I realized that I was already doing mission in my community—it didn't mean travelling somewhere else
- Helped me to share Jesus in everyday language
- I am now on the leadership team

Magnify, a new course to train estate lay pioneers, is being developed in the Diocese of Southwark, drawing upon the lessons learned in Blackburn and York. The course takes its name and its inspiration from the Magnificat and it seeks to magnify the participants' view of their God, themselves and their usefulness in God's service. Not only may working-class people have too small a view of God (and like all of us need the mind-expanding encounter with the God of the Bible), but they characteristically have too small a view of themselves. Those who have been belittled by life, often belittle themselves. *Magnify* seeks to address this directly and help the participants of the group to see themselves and their place in God's mission differently.

The *Magnify* course is designed to be the course that reaches the parts other courses do not reach. No previous qualifications or educational achievements are necessary. It consists of thirty two-hour sessions spread over a year with 6–8 participants in each local hub.

The style of learning is highly participatory and group based. There are no formal assessments or written exercises. Term one is all about *who we are in Christ.* It begins by looking at the story of our own lives, before considering what people said about Jesus and what he said about himself. It moves on to consider who we are in Christ as flawed but loved people, members of God's family, called to be fruitful in his service. Term two is about *sharing the faith.*

It begins by looking at the community the participant comes from and then how our story of faith and the story of Jesus' life can be shared with the communities where we live. Term three is about *living as an ambassador* for Christ in our communities, our families and our workplaces.

The reaction of the crowd in Acts 4 to early apostolic preaching reminds us that the first leaders of the church were ordinary working men, transformed by an encounter with Jesus:

> When they saw the courage of Peter and John and realized that they were unschooled, ordinary men, they were astonished and they took note that these men had been with Jesus. (Acts 4.13, NIV)

Unschooled, ordinary people who have been with Jesus may be the very best people to communicate the love of Jesus to people like themselves. The courses that are being pioneered in Blackburn, York, London, Birmingham, Southwark and elsewhere are designed to enable that to happen, to facilitate mission by working-class people to working-class people—and to others.

Cross-cultural Mission

The necessity for cross-cultural mission is taken for granted when Western mission partners travel overseas but it is not always realized that it is needed just as much for mission to working-class people by a predominantly middle-class church in the West. The best model for such an approach is the apostle Paul who became 'all things to all people' in order to save some (1 Cor 9.19–22, NIV).

NT Wright speaks of the 'epistemology of love' which he defines as 'entering sympathetically into the minds of people in cultures very different from our own.'[40] The key challenge for middle-class Christians engaged in mission in working-class contexts is to embrace the epistemology of love. This is not to romanticize it or to be blind to its faults but to view working-class culture *with love*. Effective cross-cultural mission amongst working-class people involves first sympathetically studying and understanding their culture, not dismissing it or diminishing it. Careful listening to working-class people is crucial. Then we need to find ways to communicate the truths of the gospel in culturally appropriate ways.

It is not difficult. It is just often not attempted.

5 Conclusion: Intentionality

Working class people are not a tiny minority. They are a large and diverse group ranging from highly skilled manual workers to the members of the so-called precariat. They are drawn from every ethnic group. They are under-represented at every level of church life.

The key challenge for the church is to engage actively with them and their culture(s), although, there is evidence that far from engaging in this field of mission, the church is actually retreating from it. Bishop Philip North at the New Wine conference in 2017 said:

> You see in the inner urban areas and outer estates of our nation there are countless people...whose lives are in a mess, who need the saving news of Jesus Christ but who will never hear it. And why not? Because there is no Christian community to proclaim, or because that community is so weak that it has given up. 'How shall they hear without a preacher?' St Paul asks in Romans chapter 10. The simple and hard truth is that, in the poorest parts of the country, we are withdrawing the preachers. The harvest is rich, but the labourers have been redeployed to wealthier areas. We are seeing the slow and steady withdrawal of church life from those communities where the poorest people in our nation live.[41]

The pattern of withdrawal needs to be reversed. The priorities of the church need to be more aligned with the upside-down values of the kingdom of God. At the annunciation, Mary sang of the king who would bring 'down rulers from their thrones' and lift up the humble (Luke 1.52–53).

It is time for the humble to be lifted up. It is time for a new movement of mission to and with working-class people. It is time for a middle-class church to intentionally engage in cross-cultural mission with working-class people. It is time to redeploy the workers to the harder areas. It is time to direct financial resources to new and creative ways of working-class mission. It is time for the church to find new ways of working alongside working-class communities. It is time for the church to invest in the overlooked and disregarded. It is time to train and equip working class Christians to take the message of God's love to their own communities and beyond. It is to time to repent of anti-working class prejudice and to find a new 'epistemology of love' that appreciates, understands, and celebrates what is good in working-class communities.

It is time to take seriously the gospel imperative to make disciples of all peoples (Matt 28.19).

And if all that seems like an almost impossible dream, it is good to remember that the founding apostles of the church were 'unschooled ordinary men' and that the first Christians were not exactly drawn from the top drawer of society:

> Brothers and sisters, think of what you were when you were called. Not many of you were wise by human standards; not many were influential; not many were of noble birth. But God chose the foolish things of the world to shame the wise; God chose the weak things of the world to shame the strong. (1 Cor 1.25–27, NIV)

Bibliography

C Arnade, *Dignity: Seeking Respect in Backrow America* (New York: Sentinel, 2019)

T Chester, *Unreached: Growing Churches in Working-class and Deprived Areas* (London: IVP, 2012)

Church Army Research Unit, *Growing Leaders on Urban Estates* (Church Army, 2023)

M Collins, *The Likes of Us: A Biography of the White Working Class* (London: Granta, 2004)

S Corbett and B Fikkert, *When Helping Hurts: How to Alleviate Poverty without Hurting the Poor and Yourself* (Chicago, IL: Moody, 2012)

P Embery, *Despised: Why the Modern Left Loathes the Working Class* (Cambridge: Polity Press, 2021)

R Gamble, *The Irrelevant Church* (London: Monarch, 1991)

D Hall, *Working Lives: The Forgotten Voices of Britain's Post-war Working Class* (Ealing: Bantam Press, 2012)

G Jenkins, *In My Place: The Spirituality of Substitution* (Grove Spirituality booklet S 71)

M McConnell and M McKinley, *Church in Hard Places* (Wheaton, IL: Crossway, 2016)

M McConnell, *The Least, the Last and the Lost* (Welwyn Garden City: Evangelical Press, 2021)

N Williams and P Brown, *Invisible Divides: Class, Culture and Barriers to Belonging in the Church* (London: SPCK, 2022)

Notes

1 *Faith in the City: A Call for Action by Church and Nation* (London: Church House Publishing, 1985).

2 *ibid*, p 28.

3 In the Church of England, for example, there has been significant General Synod debates on estates ministry in 2019 and 2024; a report has been commissioned on the experience of working-class clergy (https://www.churchofengland.org/sites/default/files/2023-10/focussed-study-4-working-class-clergy-wellbeing.pdf) and there are lay training projects for people from low income communities in a number of dioceses.

4 Some of the attributes of working-class culture described in this section are of course features of other cultures, too.

5 https://www.independent.co.uk/news/uk/home-news/britain-now-has-7-social-classes-and-working-class-is-a-dwindling-breed-8557894.html

6 https://nrs.co.uk/nrs-print/lifestyle-and-classification-data/social-grade/

7 P Embery, *Despised: Why the Modern Left Loathes the Working Class* (Cambridge: Polity, 2021) p 14.

8 https://www.spiked-online.com/2022/11/05/the-future-belongs-to-blue-labour/

9 N Williams and P Brown, *Invisible Divides: Class, Culture and Barriers to Belonging in the Church* (London: SPCK, 2022) p 17.

10 *Living Ministry Focussed Study 4, 'Let justice roll down like waters': Exploring the Wellbeing of Working-Class Clergy in the Church of England: A Rally Cry for Change,* Church of England Ministry Development Team, 2023, p 33.

11 Let the reader understand: I am not suggesting *all* working-class people hold these views but many do. For example, it is estimated that 64% of working-class people voted for Britain to leave the European Community: https://www.statista.com/statistics/518395/brexit-votes-by-social-class/

12 See my article on Ian Paul's blog: https://www.psephizo.com/life-ministry/where-are-the-working-class/

13 P Embery, *Despised, op cit*, p 14.

14 Sadly we must note that has not always been the case. We must mourn the lack of welcome and outright racism and rejection that was offered to black Christians moving to the UK.

15 An interesting regional variation: the use of the word 'babe' is particularly characteristic of *south* Londoners. See 'the blokes will call everyone babe' https://metro.co.uk/2015/09/03/21-ways-to-spot-a-real-londoner-5364416/

16 Indeed, at least one speaker warned the synod of the dangers of elitism and in due course the terms of the debate and the final motion were widened somewhat.

17 S Corbett and B Fikkert, *When Helping Hurts: How to Alleviate Poverty without Hurting the Poor and Yourself* (Chicago, IL: Moody, 2012) p 51.

18 R D Lupton, *Toxic Charity: How Churches and Charities Hurt Those they Help (and How to Reverse it)* (San Francisco, CA: HarperOne, 2011) p 128.

19 https://www.stlyrics.com/lyrics/josephandtheamazingtechnicolordreamcoat/onemoreangelinheaven.htm

20 C Arnade, *Dignity: Seeking Respect in Backrow America* (New York: Sentinel, 2019) pp 112–113.

21 L Newbigin, *The Gospel in a Pluralist Society* (Grand Rapids, MI: Eerdmans, 1989) p 227.

22 G Jenkins, *In My Place: the Spirituality of Substitution* (Grove Spirituality booklet S 71).

23 *ibid*, p 16.

24 https://www.churchofengland.org/about/vision-strategy/estates-evangelism/estates-evangelism

25 C Arnade, *Dignity, op cit*, p 112.

26 *ibid*, pp 120–122.

27 N Williams and P Brown, *Invisible Divides: Class, Culture and Barriers to Belonging in the Church* (London: SPCK, 2022) p 9.

28 https://jesusshapedpeople.net/programmes/jsp

29 https://www.leadingyourchurchintogrowth.org.uk/the-start-course

30 https://www.eden.co.uk/christian-books/spiritual-growth/evangelism-and-followup/simply-christianity-leaders-manual/

31 http://www.urbanministries.org.uk/catechism.html

32 https://proximityhub.org/

33 All the videos may be viewed on the St James and St Anne, Bermondsey YouTube page.

34 N Williams and P Brown, *Invisible Divides, op cit*, p 138.

35 Church Army Research Unit, *Growing Leaders on Urban Estates* (Church Army, 2023) p 3.

36 *ibid*.

37 *ibid*, p 9.

38 *ibid*, p 10.

39 Church Army Research Unit, *Growing Leaders on Urban Estates, op cit.*

40 https://www.firstthings.com/article/2020/02/loving-to-know

41 https://www.blackburn.anglican.org/storage/general-files/shares/Resources/Talks%20articles%20and%20sermons/Hope_for_the_Poor_-__P_article__Word_document_.pdf